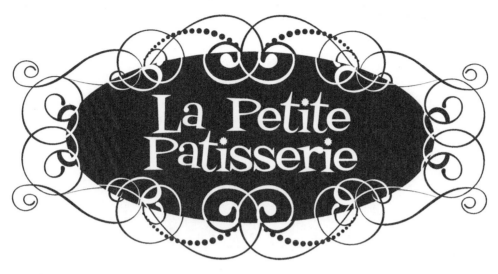

La Petite Patisserie

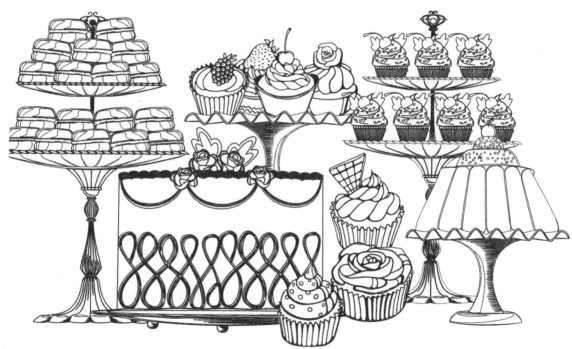

Really Cool Colouring **Book 3**

First published in 2015 by Kyle Craig Publishing

Text and illustration copyright © 2015 Kyle Craig Publishing

Editor: Alison McNicol

Design: Julie Anson

ISBN: 978-1-908-707-53-6

A CIP record for this book is available from the British Library.

A Kyle Craig Publication

www.kyle-craig.com

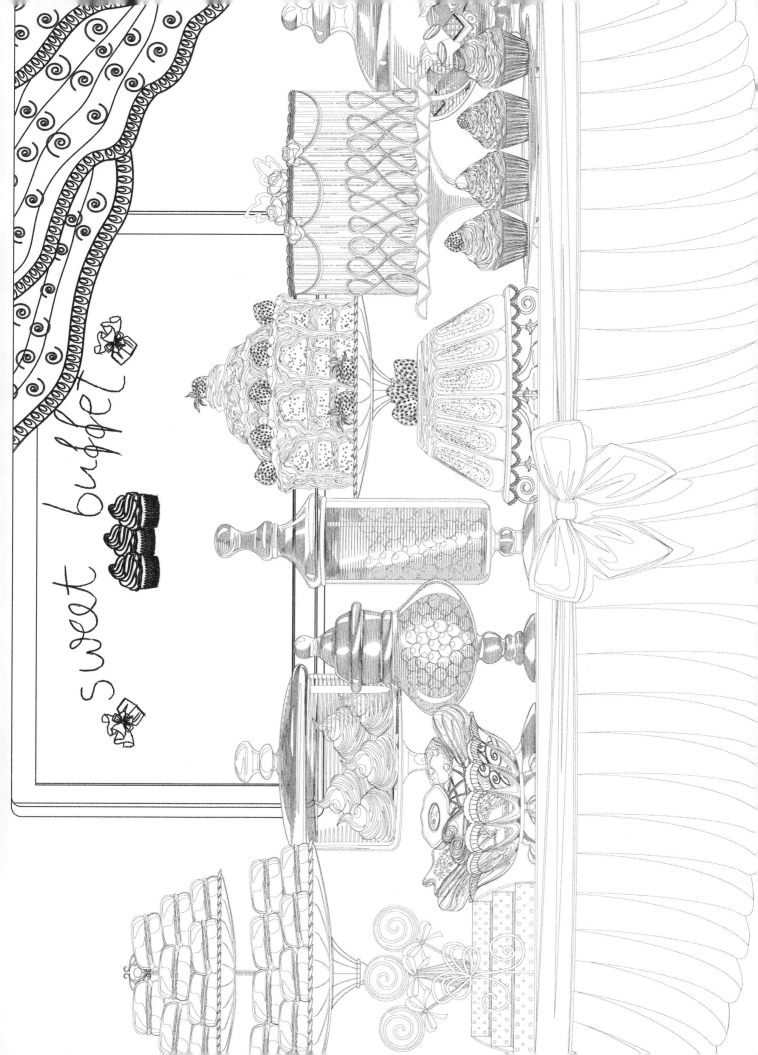

sweet buffet

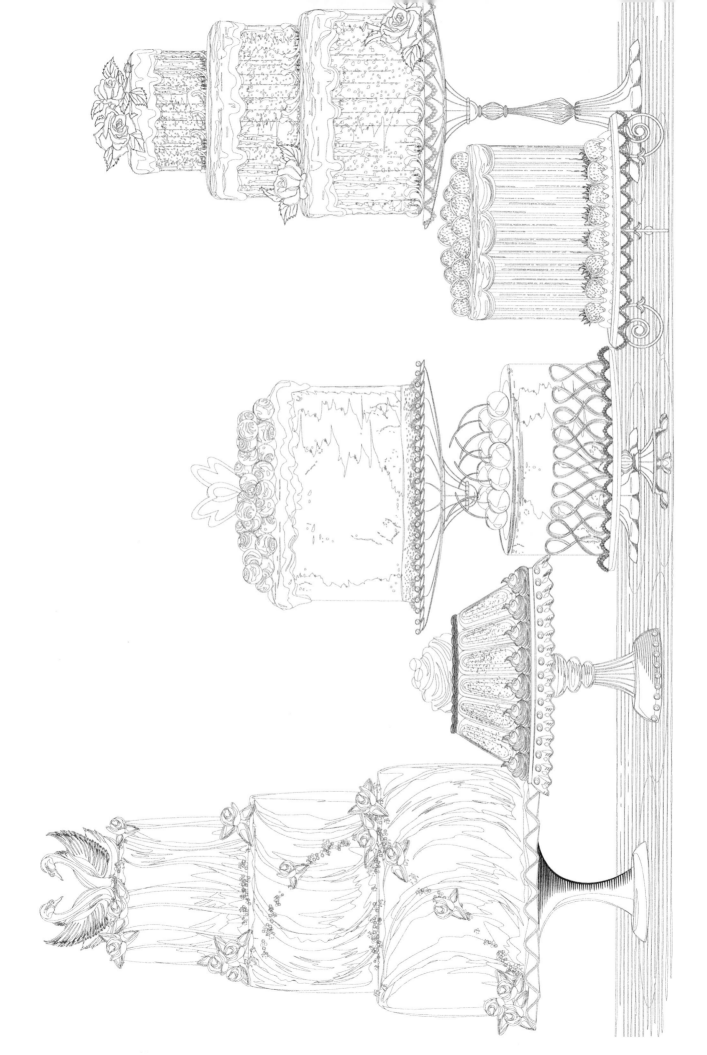

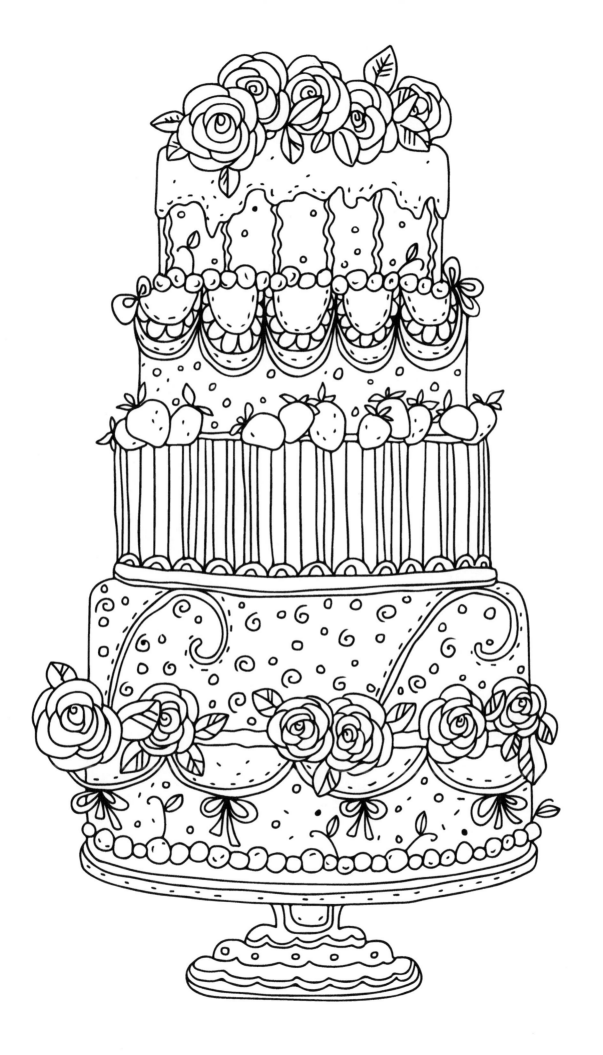

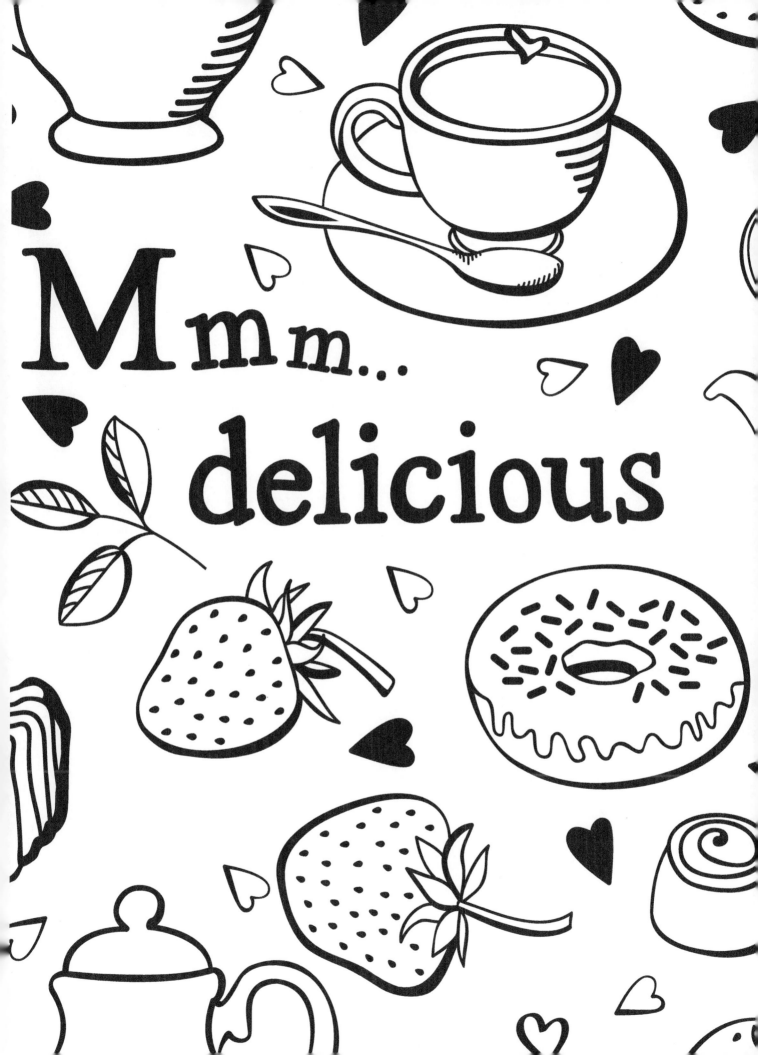

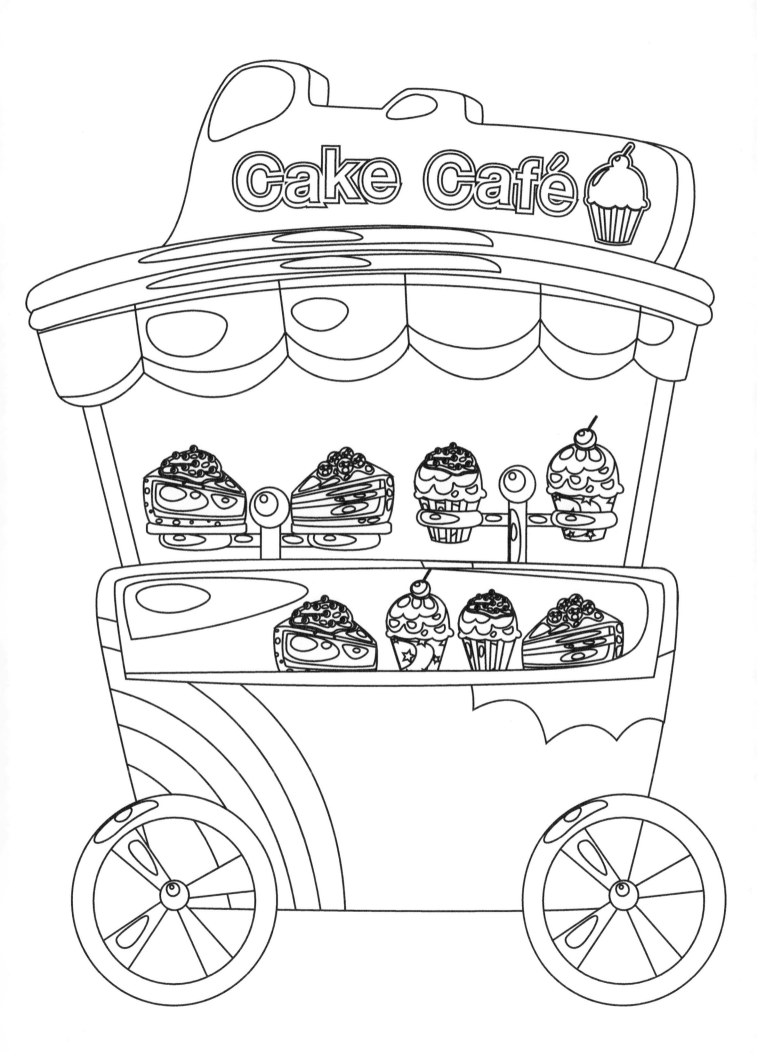

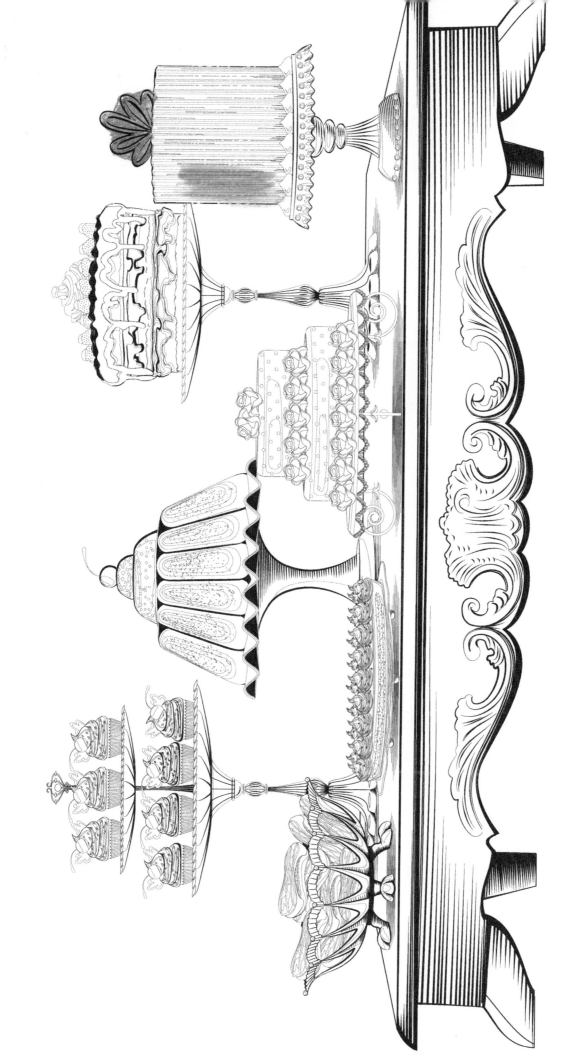

Hand Decorated

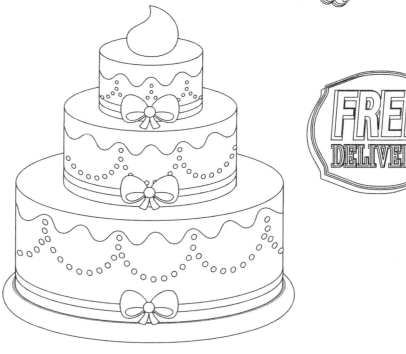

FREE DELIVERY

CAKES

AND DESSERTS

Made With Love

SINCE 1973

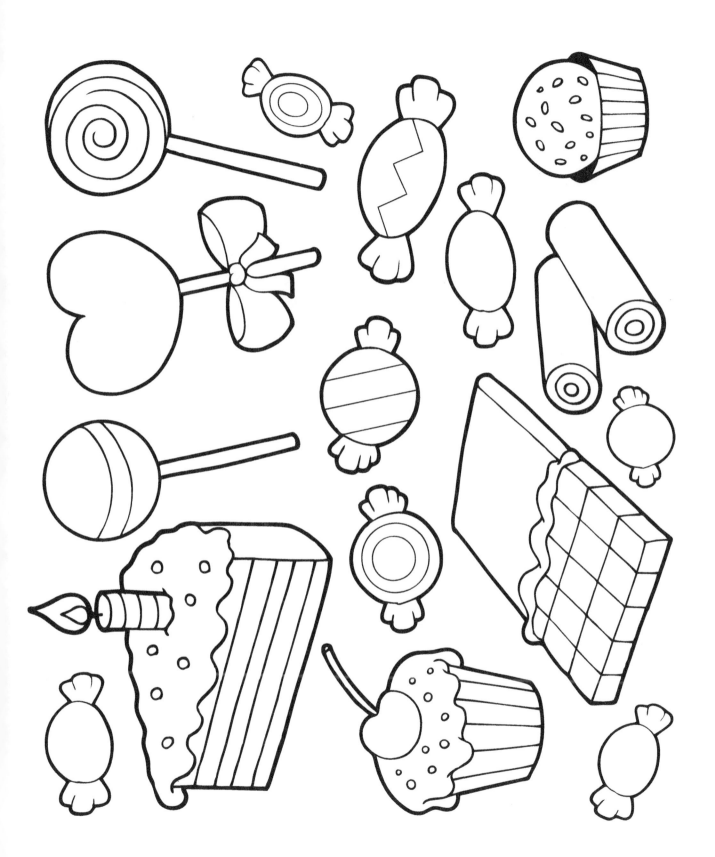

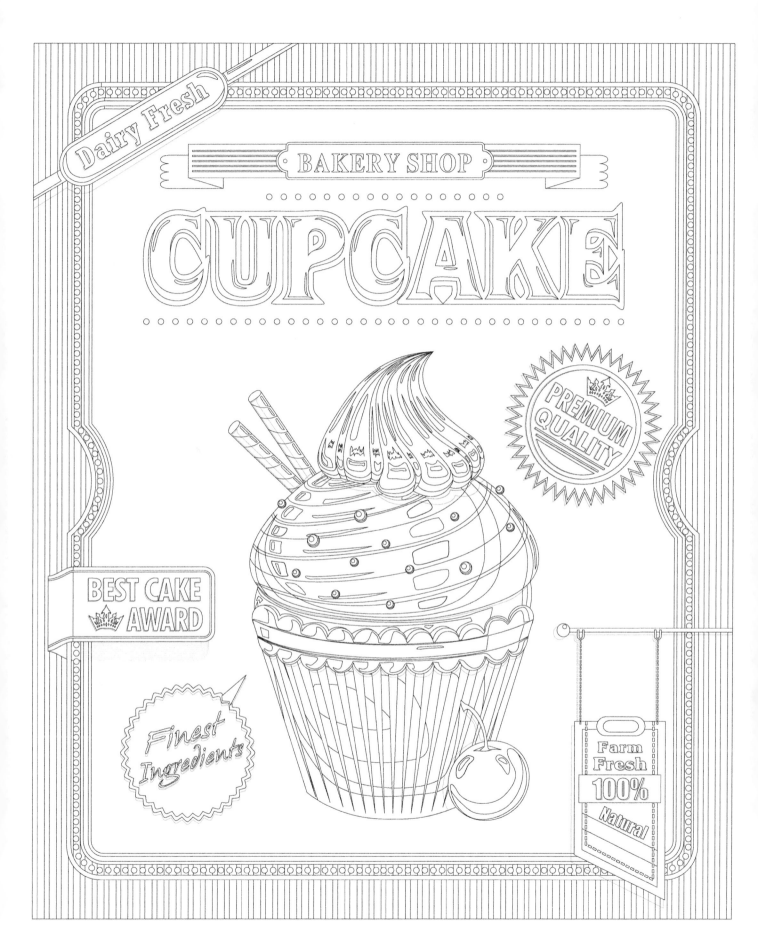

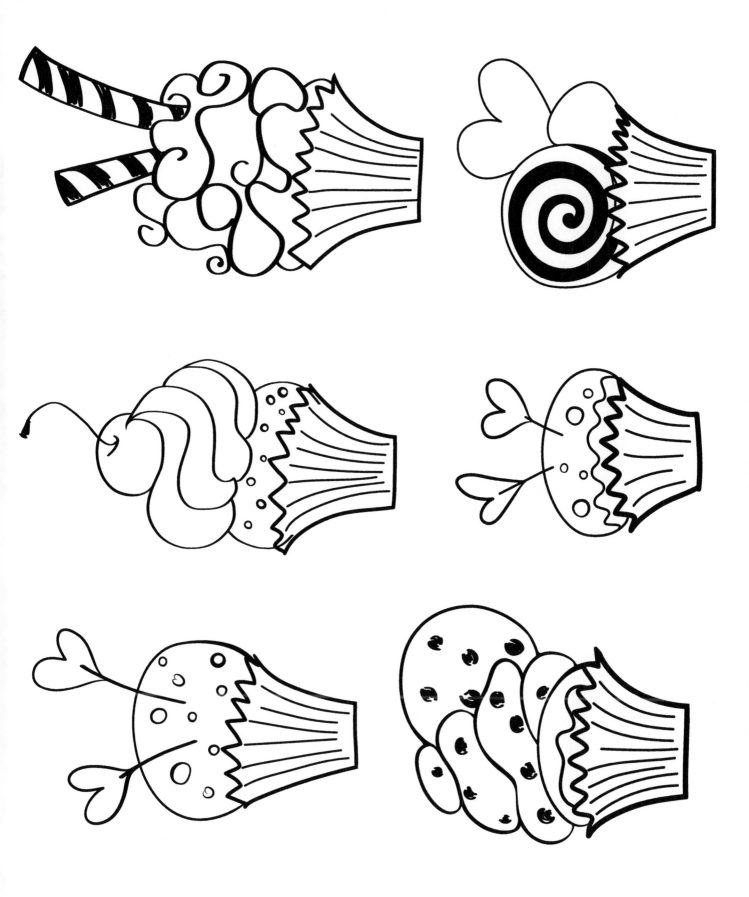

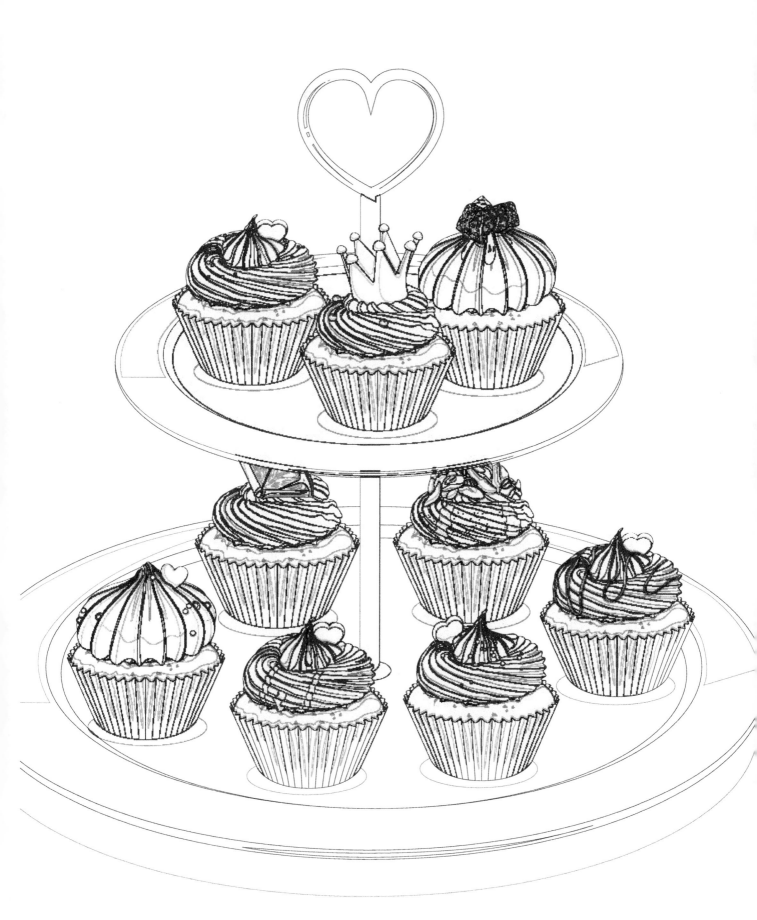

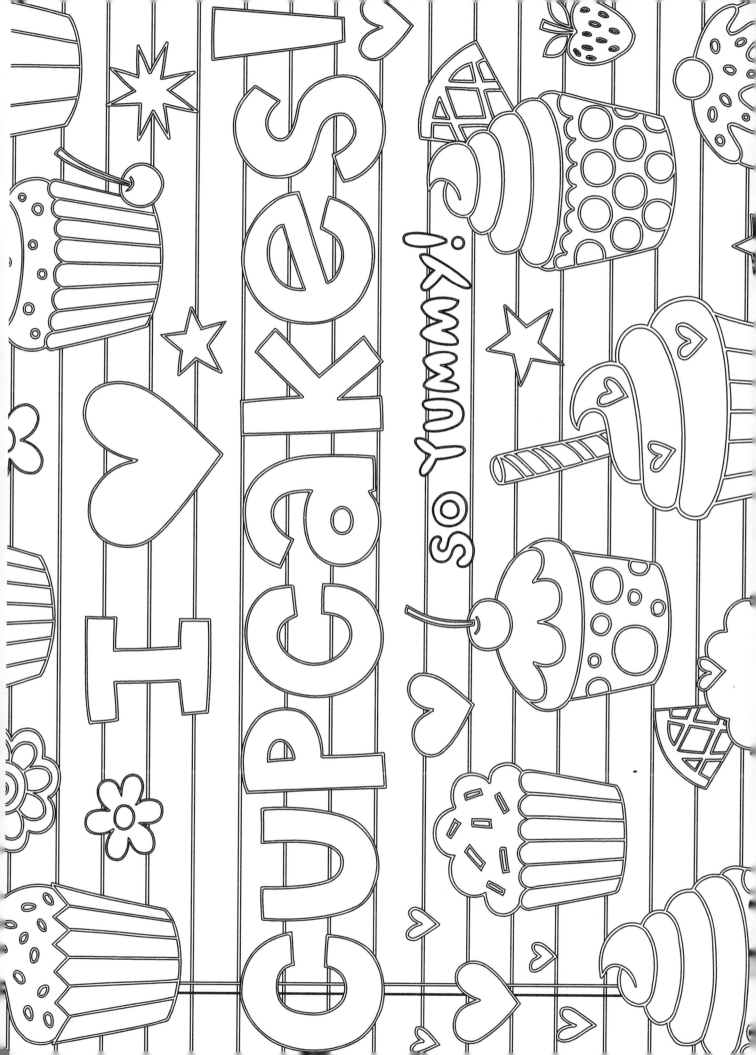

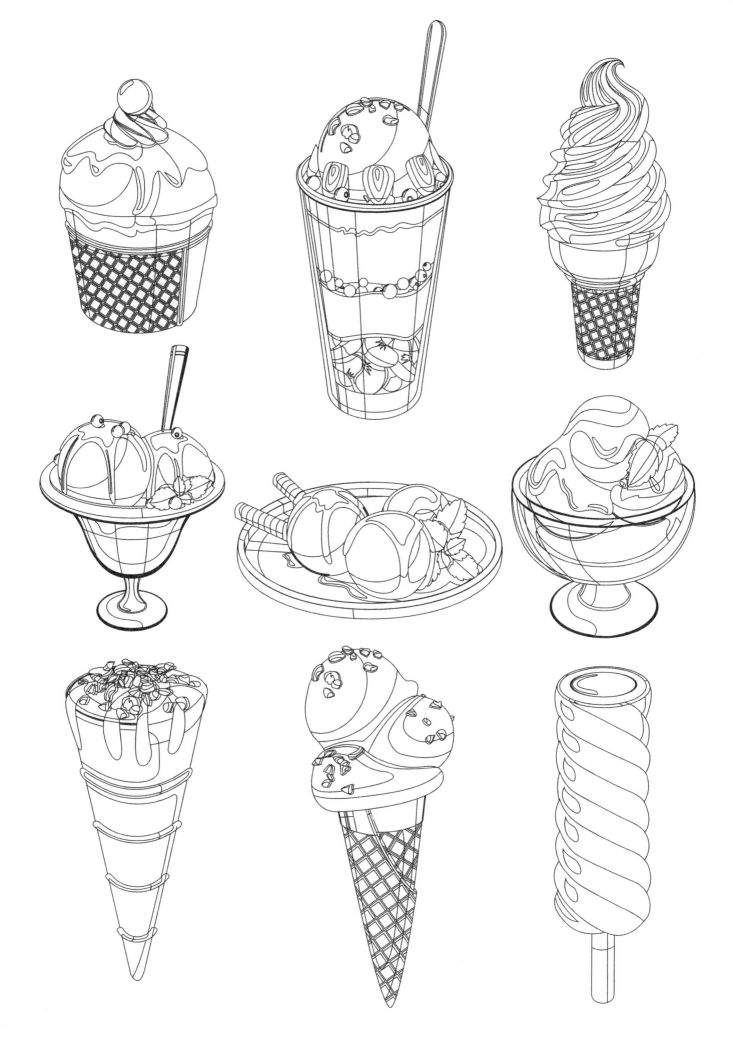

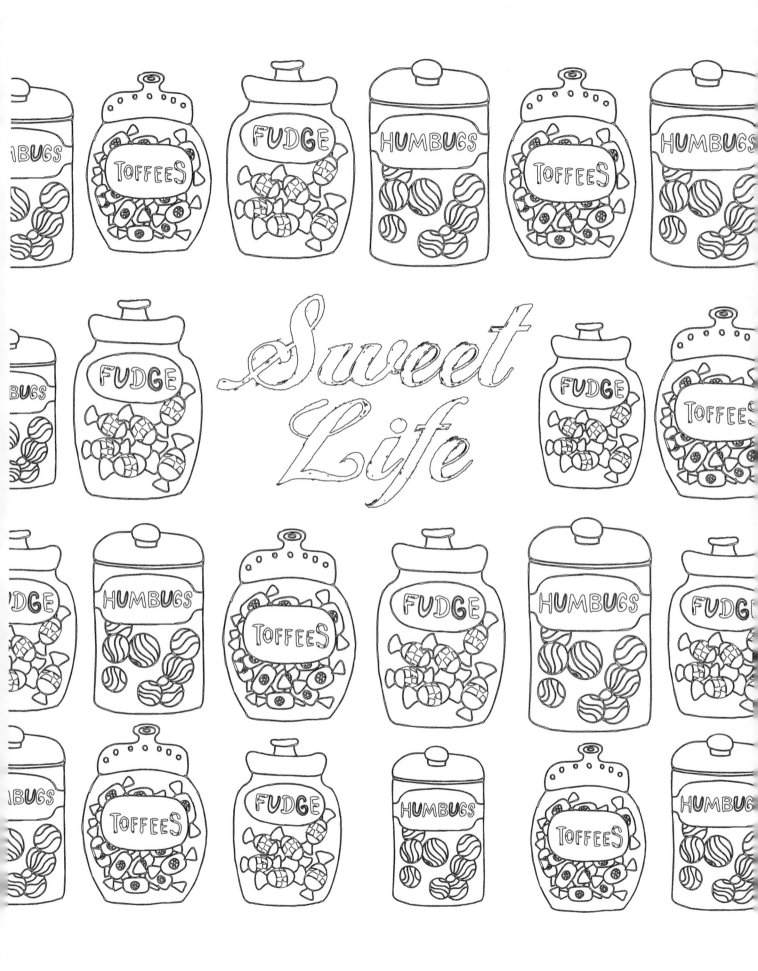

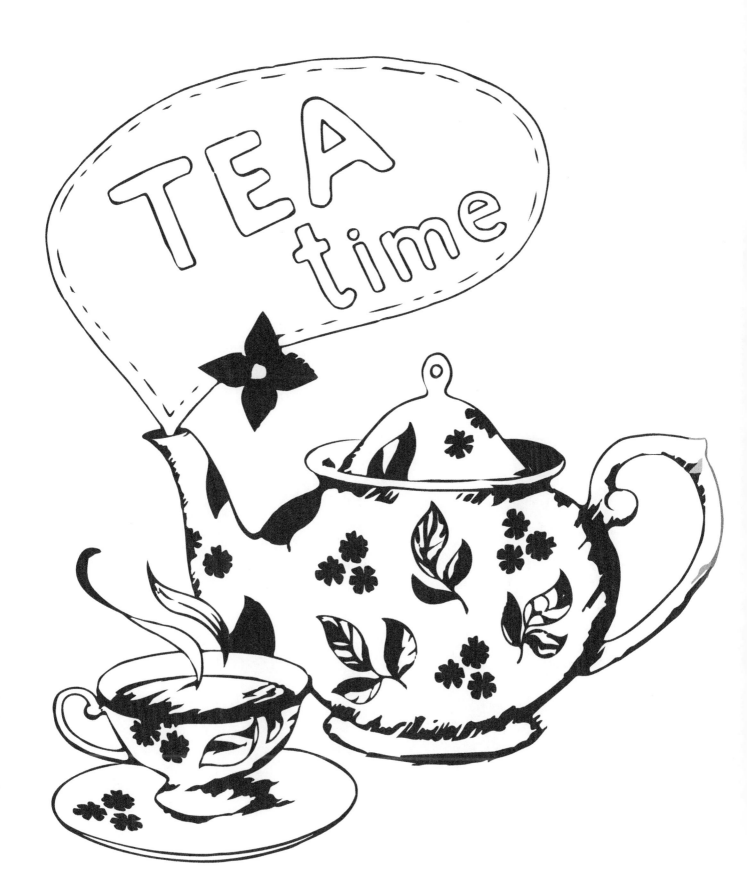

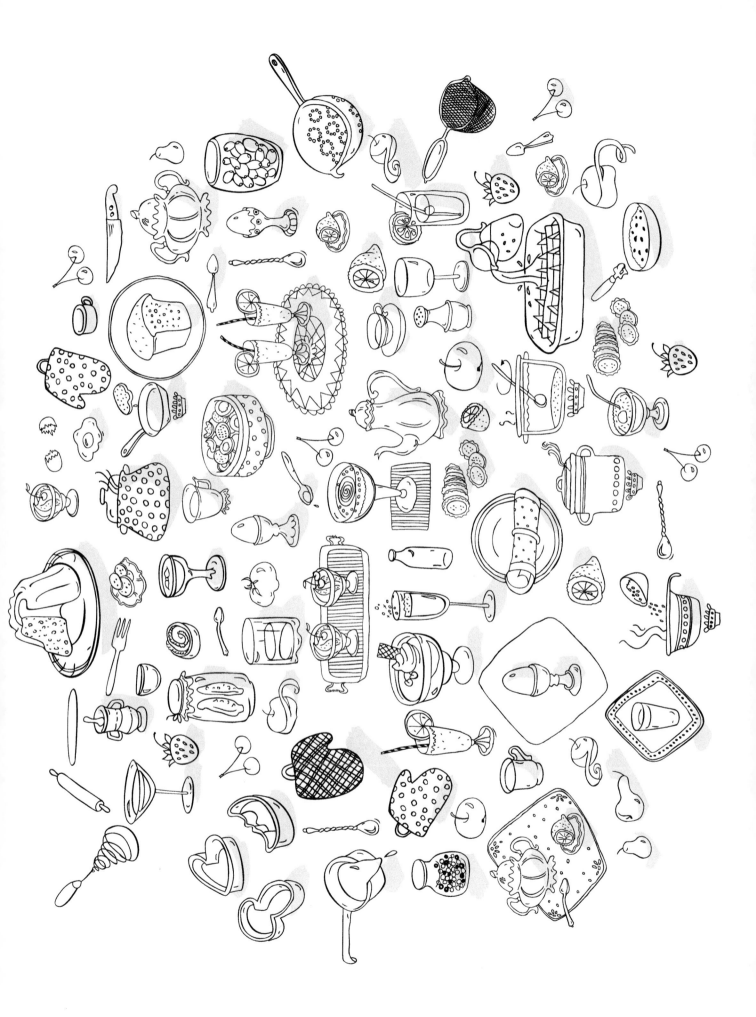

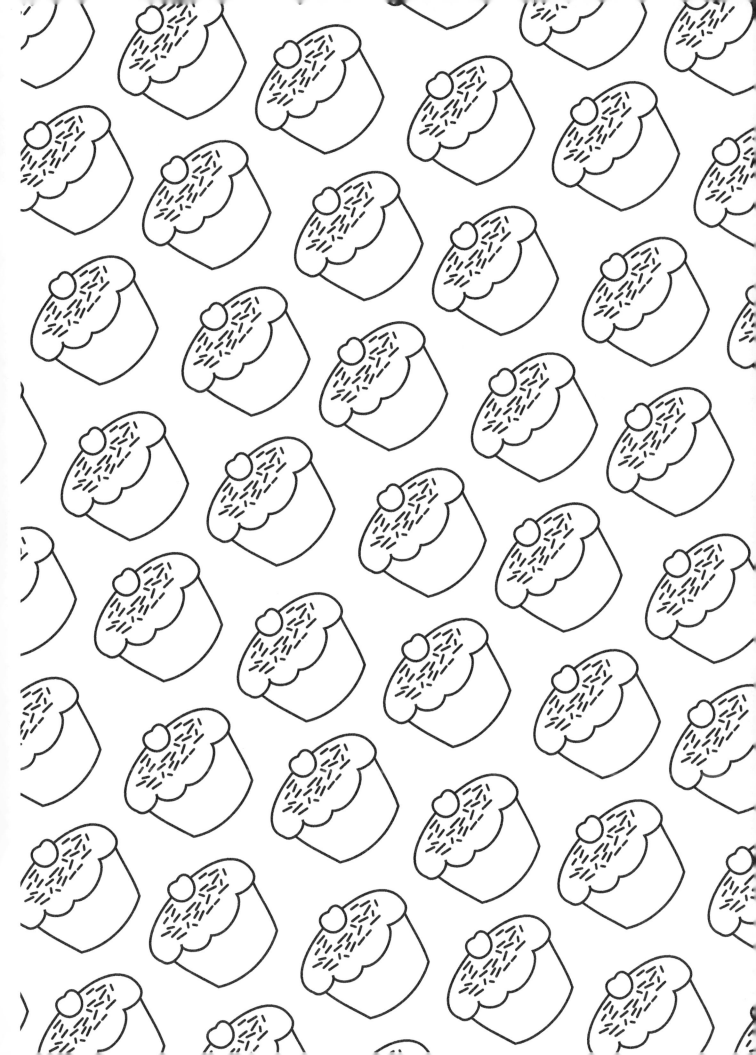

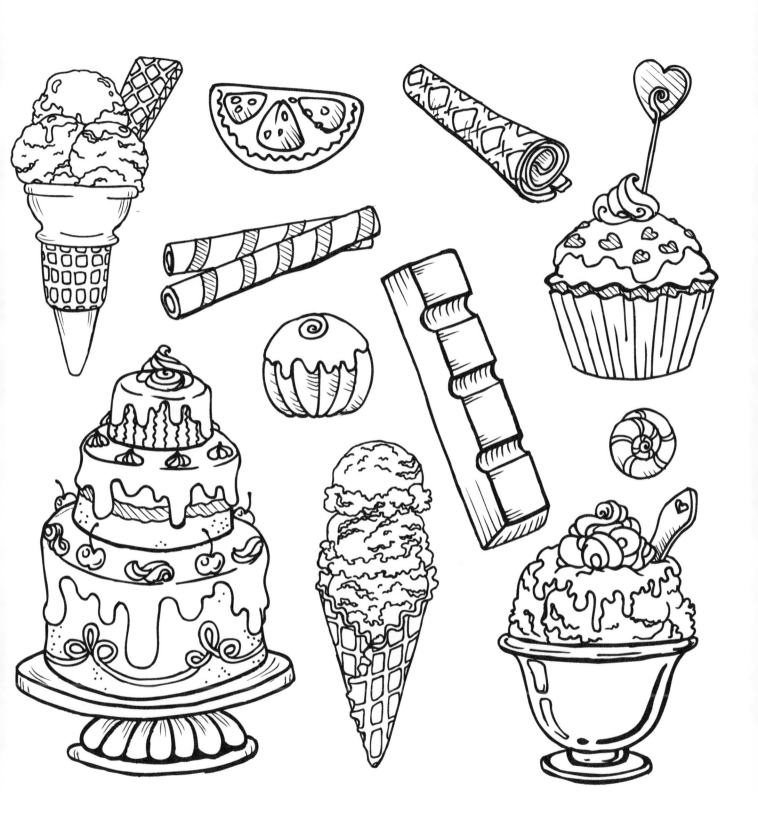

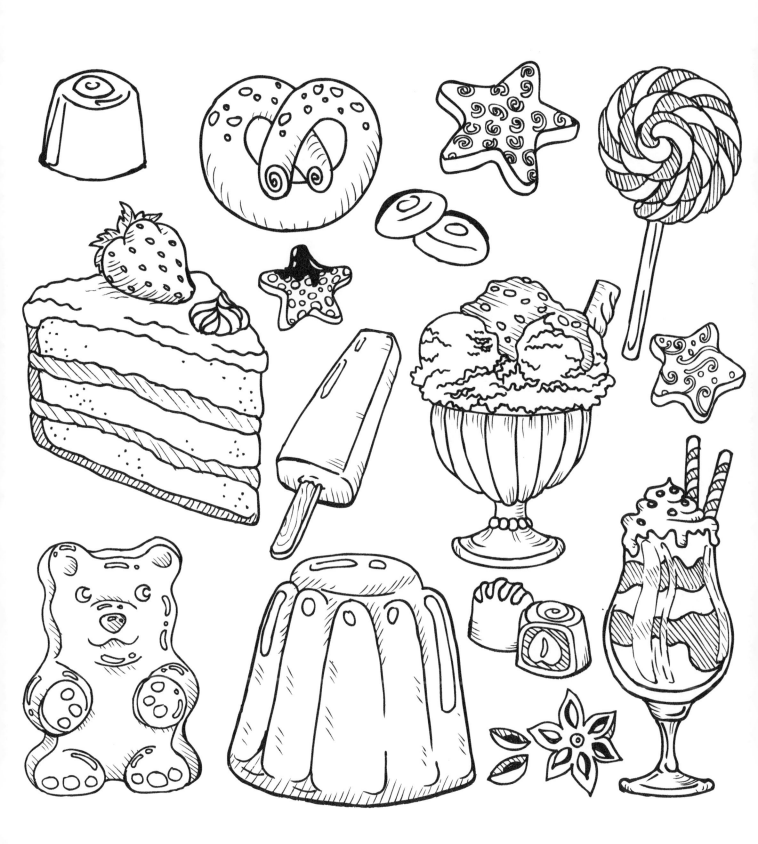

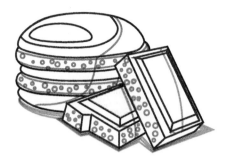

White chocolate

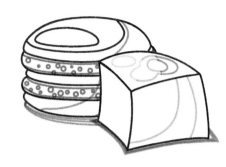

Creme Brulee

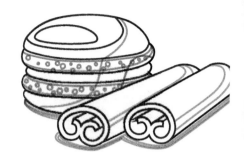

Cinnamon

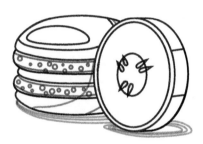

Banana

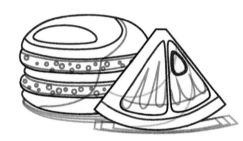

Lemon

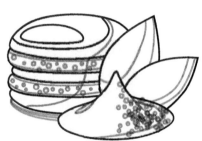

Matcha

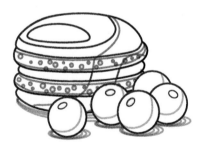

Blueberry

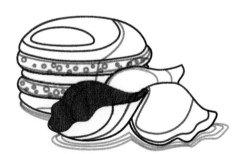

Rose

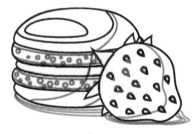

Strawberry

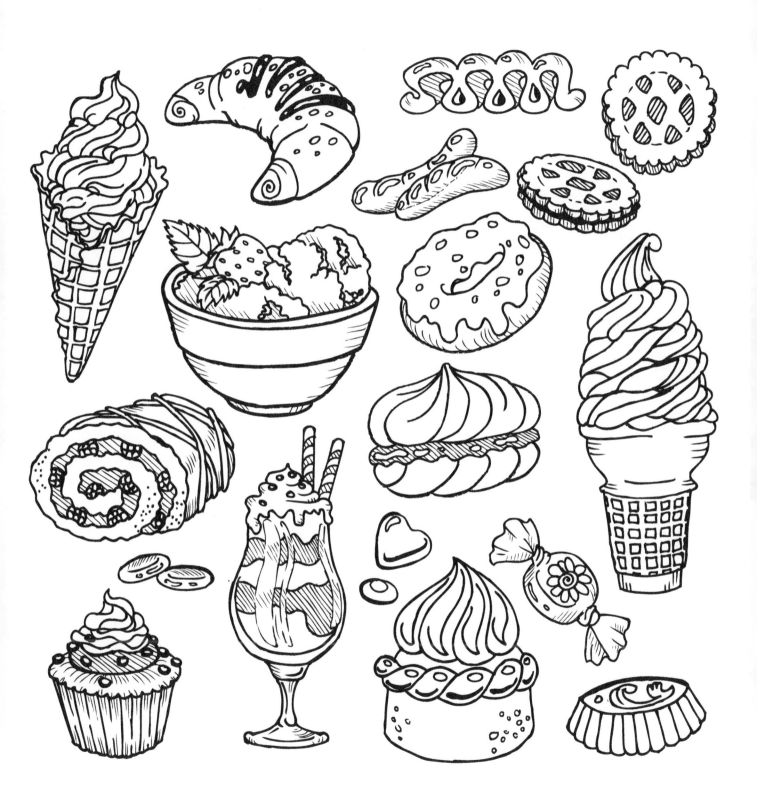

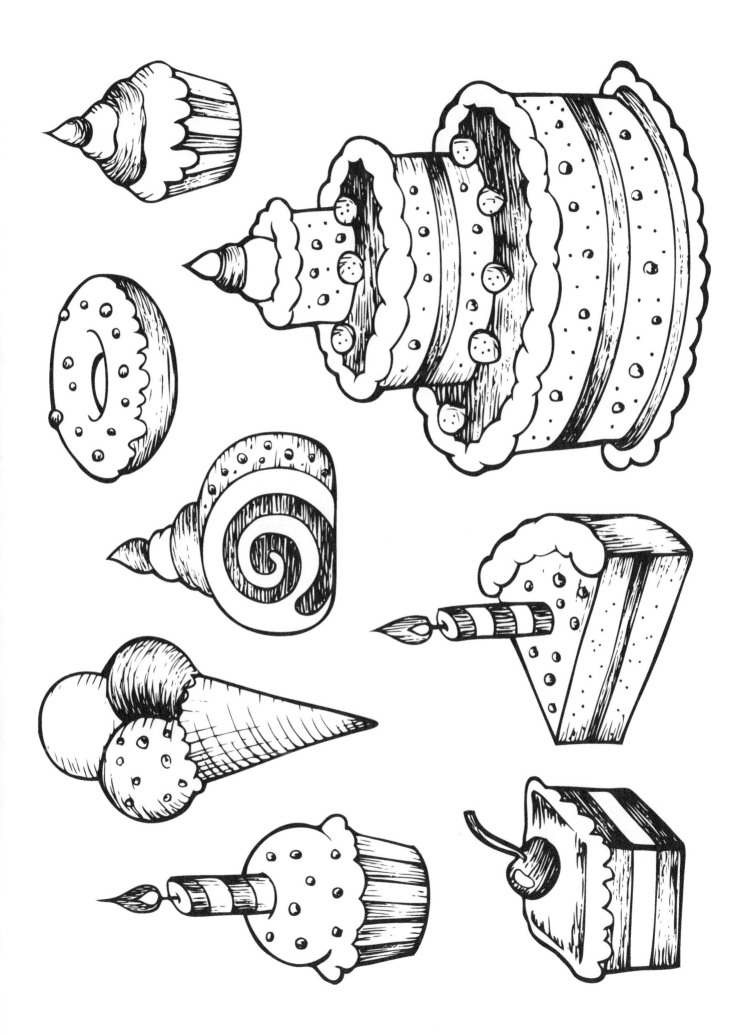

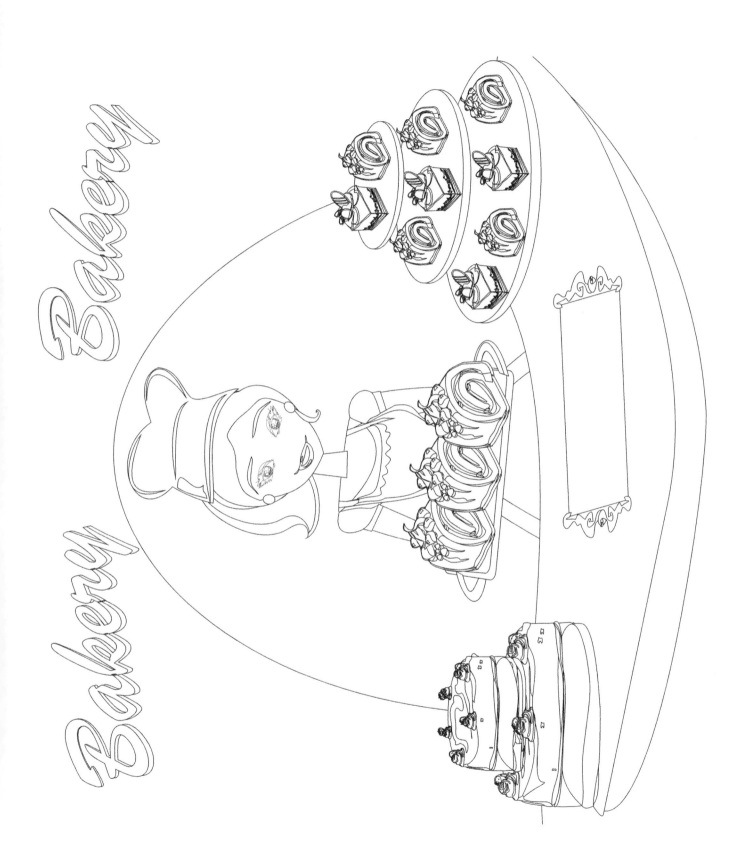

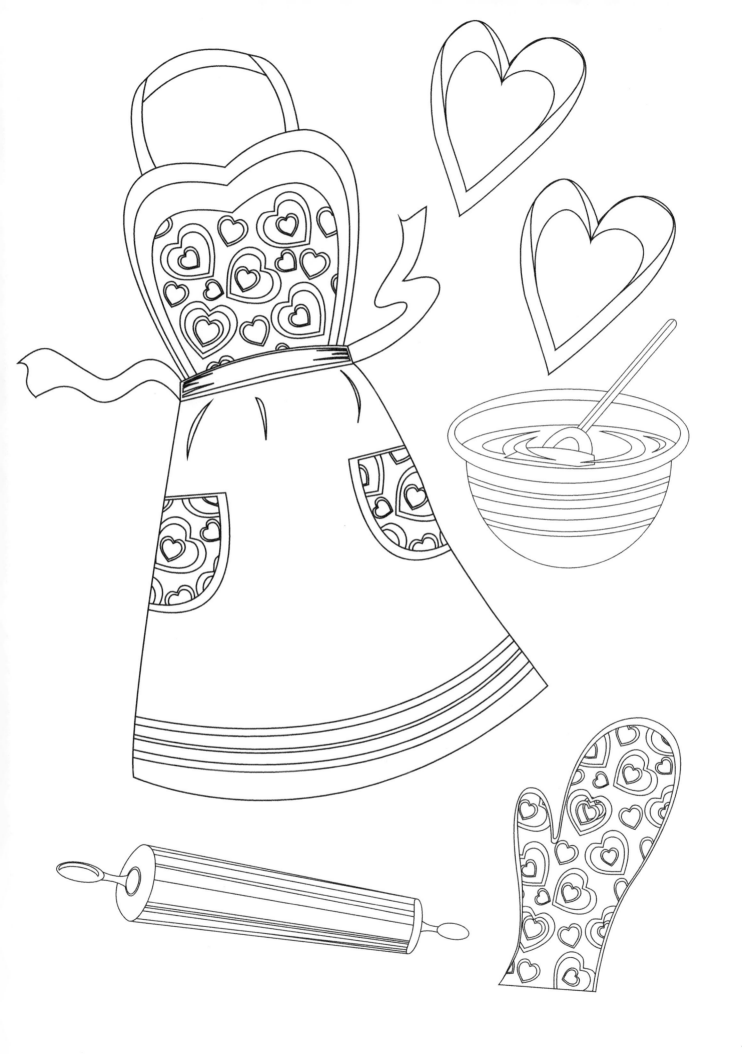

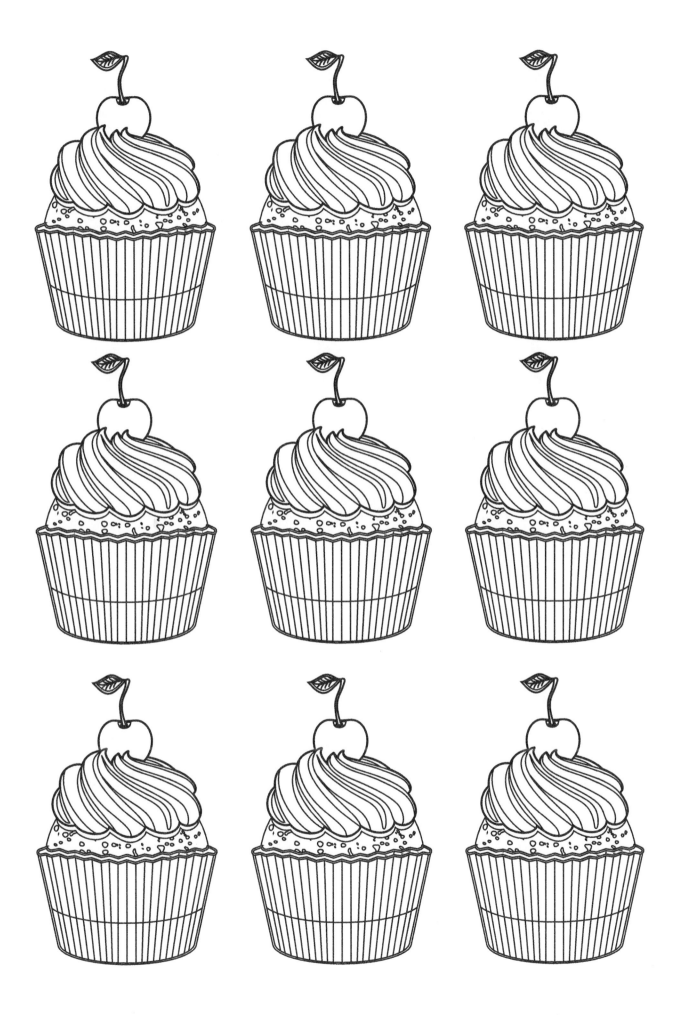

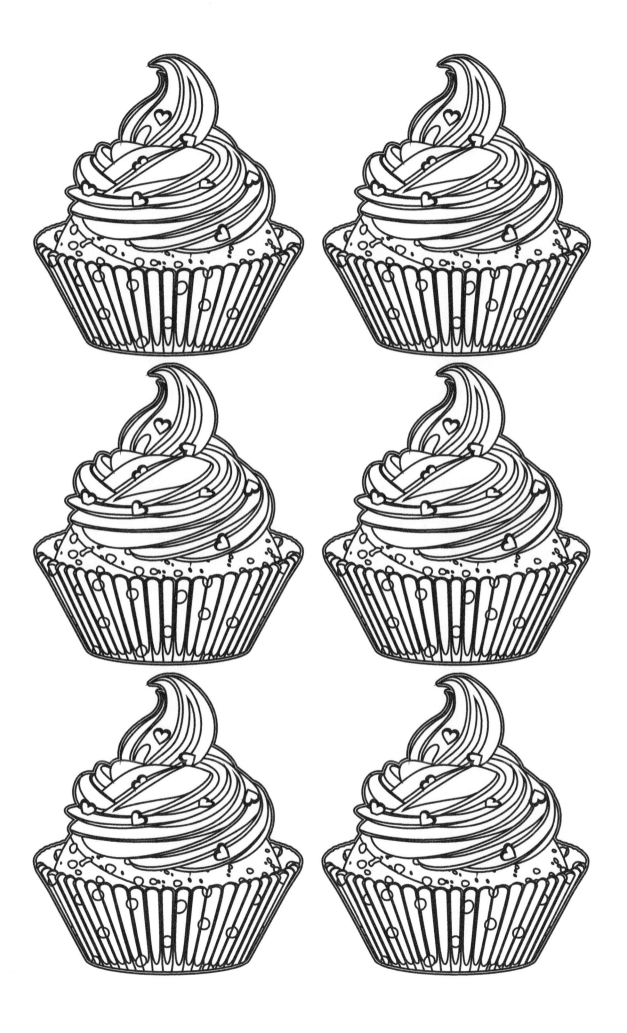

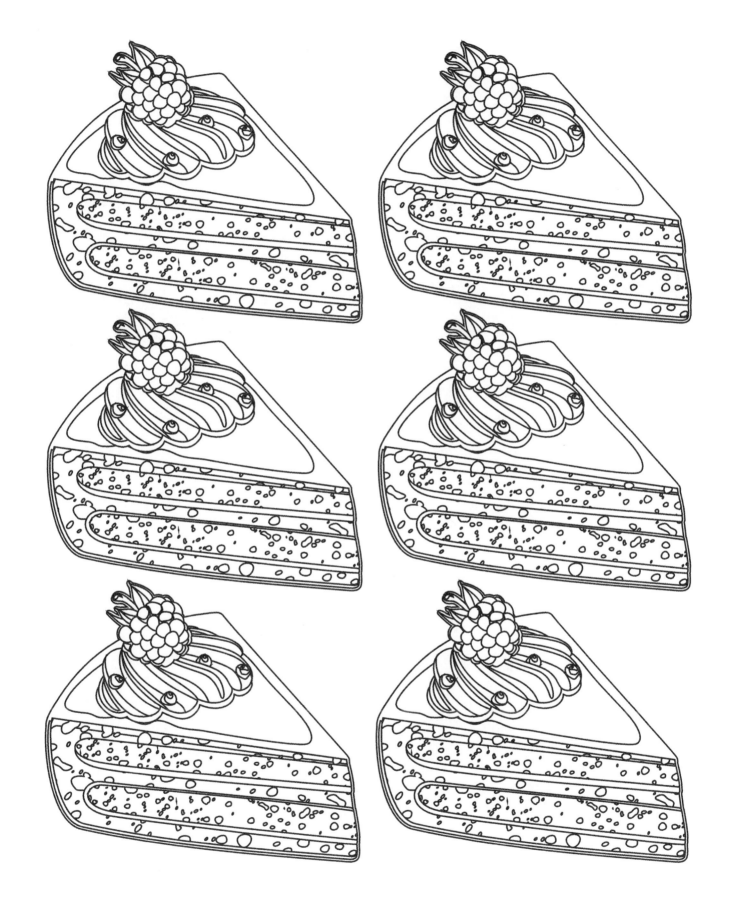

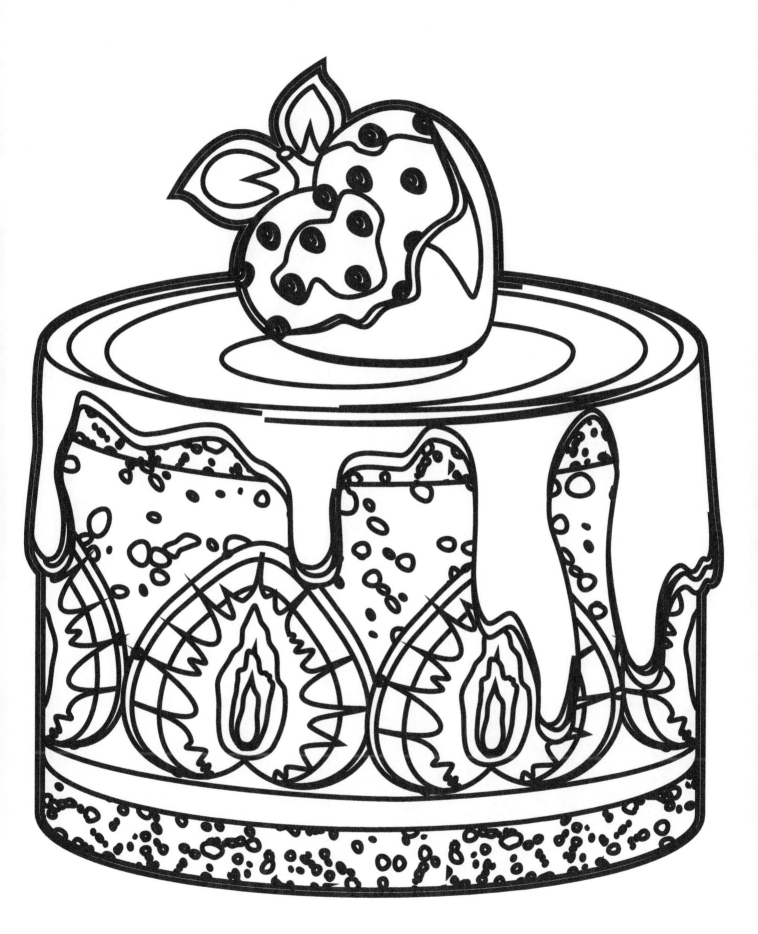

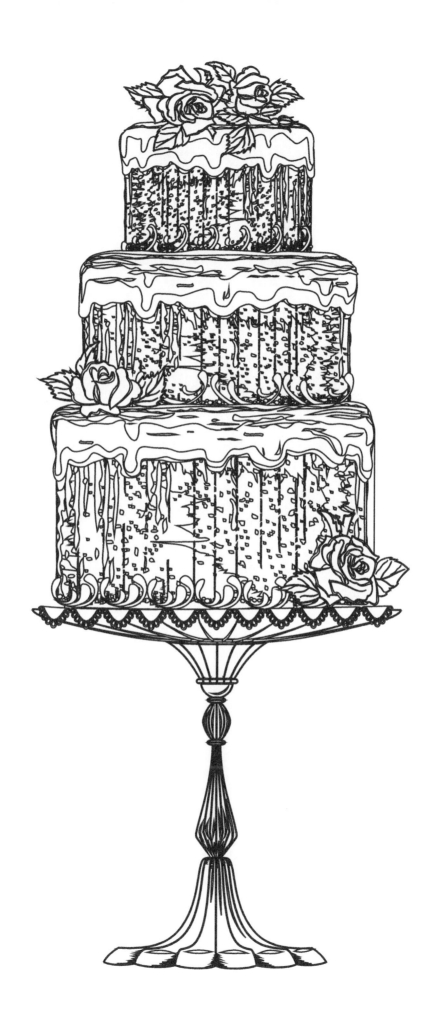

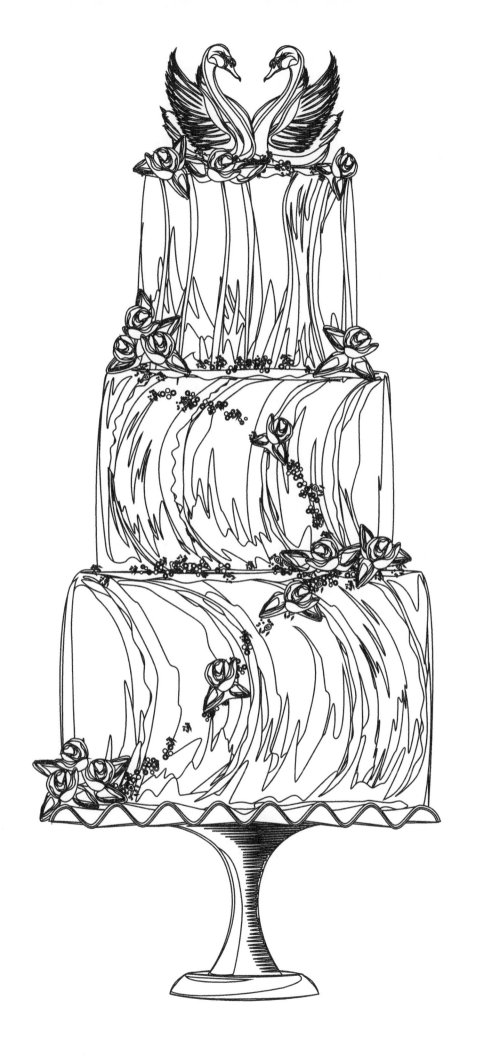

Printed in Great Britain
by Amazon